Copyright © 2017 by Lenn Vincent GmbH.

All rights reserved. This book or any portion thereof may not be reproduced or used in any manner whatsoever without the express written permission of the publisher except for the use of brief quotations in a book review.

First Printing, 2017

ISBN 978-3-9524827-6-6

www.leosnowpard.com

Leo Snowpard
AND THE TOY EXCHANGE PROJECT

Author
MELANIE ROEMER

Illustrations by
JUN-PIERRE SHIOZAWA

Leo Snowpard is already in second grade and loves school, most of the time at least. Mrs. Smith, his teacher, always plans great projects with the children. Today the project is about a time when there was no money and things were exchanged.

"A long time ago, people had no money. Nevertheless, at that time, they were not allowed to take what they liked. People had to exchange things."

"How did they exchange things?" asked Leo. "They might have exchanged eggs for flour or milk for butter, for example."

"Like when I exchange my cheese bread with Maya's yogurt?" Leo asks.

"Correct, Leo," Mrs. Smith affirmed.

"But people had to have something to trade to get the things they wanted to exchange. Do you know what you need, for example, to have chicken eggs?"
"You need chickens," Maya replied. "And you need a chicken stall," says Elli Elephant. "That's right. And you have to feed the chickens daily, clean the barn, collect eggs, and so on," Mrs. Smith explains.
Leo thought. "And then you can get whatever you wanted for one egg?"

"Not quite. For small things you needed less eggs and for big things people had to collect many eggs. Or Leo, would you exchange your cheese sandwich for one of Maya's strawberries?" Mrs. Smith smiled at Leo.

"Hmm I do not know… I love strawberries but then I would still be hungry," Leo and his classmates laugh.

"I agree! You should only exchange your sandwich with something that can fill you up. If you find that, you have found a suitable exchange partner," Mrs. Smith explains.

Leo has an idea. "How about exchanging our toys?"
Mrs. Smith smiles. The other children murmur with each other and agree with the proposal. Maya continues: "Oh yes, that could be our Toy Exchange Project. Everyone bring toys, which they would like to exchange and then look for an exchange partner!" The classmates like the idea. Together, they decide to start the project next Monday. Mrs. Smith writes the date and the task onto the homework board and then the school bell rings. "So think about exchanging toys and have a great weekend," Mrs. Smith says to the children.

The weekend passes by in no time and Leo has a lot of fun. In the evening before school, Leo sits with Lilly on the sofa and they talk with each other. "Lilly, tomorrow we will have our own Toy Exchange Project at school. We exchange our toys among each other."

"That sounds exciting. What are you going to take?" Suddenly, Leo encounters the fact that he has not yet picked out any toys for the Toy Exchange Project. "Come Lilly, I have to collect toys." Leo takes Lilly by the hand and walks with her into his nursery.

Leo looks at his toys. "Oh look Lilly, my toy train. Let's build it up!" Leo forgets what he actually wanted to do. Lilly gets impatient. "Look Leo, you have not played with the car for a long time. Can I put it in your backpack?"
"No, it's my car, I like to play with it," Leo takes the car from Lilly and puts it back. Leo would like to keep all the toys. But he also remembered that he wanted to exchange something at school. That is why he begins to put the toys, which he has not played with for a long time into his backpack. So grows curious wondering what he can exchange his well-loved toys for at school the next day.

The next day, Leo arrives early to school. Mrs. Smith has already prepared the class for the project. Two children share a table and can lay out their toys. The children distribute their toys on the tables.

"What beautiful toys," Leo thinks. "It's like a toy store!" Leo immediately noticed a money box that he likes. The money box is from Kimmy crocodile. Leo takes his car and runs to Kimmy. "Hey look, I would like to exchange your money box for my car," Leo takes the money box. But Kimmy takes it back. "No, Leo."

Kimmy runs to Maya and looks at her teddy bear. "I'd love to exchange my money box with your teddy bear!", Kimmy holds her money box to Maya to exchange for her teddy.

Maya has an idea. She noticed that Leo wanted the money box. "How about if you take my teddy bear, I take Leo's car and Leo gets your money box?" Maya looks at the two smiling and winks at Leo. "Okay, so we'll do it like this!"

Leo, Maya, and Kimmy are all very happy. They agreed and found the right exchange partner.

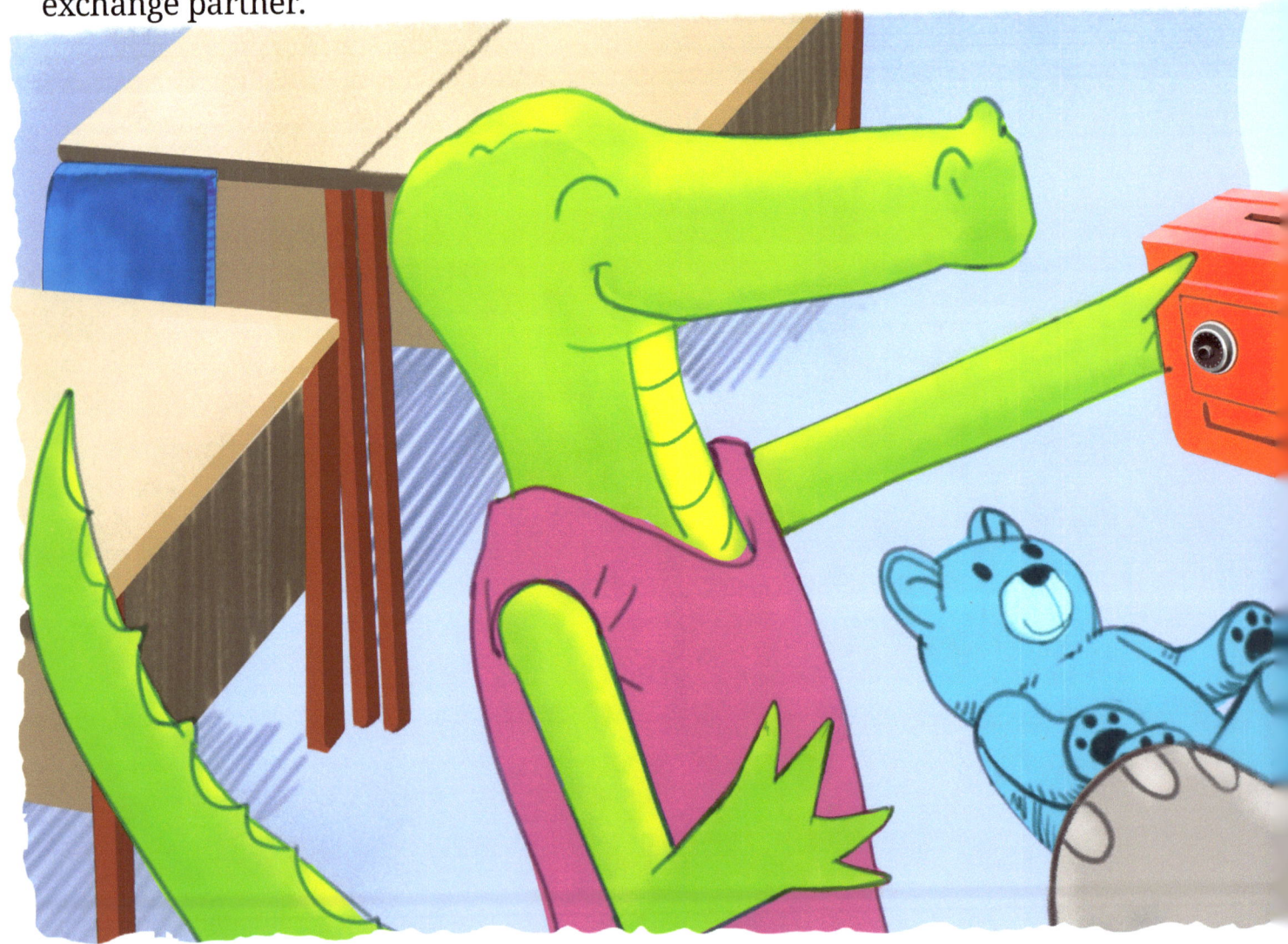

Mrs. Smith calls the children together. "So, kids, did you like the Toy Exchange Project?" All the children cheer an enthusiastic "Yes!"
"Well, then, tell me what you learned from the Exchange-Toys-Project?"
Kimmy Krokodil starts, "Back in the old days, people did not have any money. At the time, they were looking for exchange partners to exchange things." Elli Elefant continues, "It's not easy to exchange things with each other. You have to talk a lot to each other until you find the right exchange partner." Leo continues, "And sometimes someone wants to exchange something the other does not like. And then you do not exchange anything." "That's all correct," said Mrs. Smith.

"And how is it today?" asks Kimmy crocodile. "Today, we are exchanging things with money," explains Mrs. Smith. "When we go into a store, we exchange our money for things like toys. The shopkeeper gets money and we get the toys in return."

Leo wants to know more. "And where do we get the money from?"

"Good question, Leo. Instead of keeping chickens to exchange the eggs, one goes today to work to make money. With this money, we will then exchange what we need and want," explains Mrs. Smith.

At the end of the day, the children are very tired. It is exhausting to exchange. Leo got a lot of new toys, but also kept some of his toys. He is happy with what he has exchanged. Cheerful, he goes home and looks forward to the next great school project!

www.ingramcontent.com/pod-product-compliance
Lightning Source LLC
Chambersburg PA
CBHW040034050426
42453CB00003B/113

*9 7 8 3 9 5 2 4 8 2 7 6 6 *